WORCESTE
PRIVI

by

ALAN RICHARDS

COUNTRYSIDE BOOKS

NEWBURY · BERKSHIRE

First published 1999
© Alan Richards 1999

COUNTRYSIDE BOOKS
3 Catherine Road
Newbury, Berkshire

ISBN 1 85306 540 4

*For my youngest grandchildren: Josh, James, Rachel and Olivia,
the nincompoopers who made me privy to their
lavatorial language and laughter*

Produced through MRM Associates Ltd., Reading
Typeset by Techniset Typesetters, Merseyside
Printed by Woolnough Bookbinding Ltd., Irthlingborough

CONTENTS

FOREWORD

I have two small grandsons aged 3 and 5 whose most stinging insults to each other consist of a mixture of the following words: wee, bum, potty, willy, stinkbomb, poo, ponger, pooper and, more recently, nincompooper. I suspect that the appeal of Winnie the Pooh/Pooh Bear for them lies mainly in his lavatorial name. This extensive usage of terms for the body's natural functions by very young children seems to begin as soon as they can talk, and in the adult world of 1990s' Hollywood films, like the *Diehard* series, there is a similar obsession and the expressive four letter Anglo-Saxon words for our bodily functions seem to make up most of the repetitive dialogue. The use of euphemisms for the blunter words in other circles, however, is beautifully summed up in the following ode first published in *The Limerick: A Facet of Our Culture* by A. R. Morse:

> When Ladies, God bless 'em, are milling about,
> You may wee-wee, make water, or empty the glass;
> You can powder your nose; even 'Johnnie' may pass;
> Shake the dew off the lily, see the man 'bout the dog,
> Or when everyone's soused, it's 'condensing the fog'.
> But please to remember if you would know bliss
> That only in Shakespeare do characters ----.
> You may speak of a 'movement' or sit on a seat,
> Have a passage or stool – or simply excrete,
> Or say to the others, 'I'm going out in back',
> And groan in pure joy in that smelly old shack.
> You can go 'lay a cable' or do 'number two'
> Or sit on the toidey and make a 'do-do',
> But ladies and men who are socially fit
> Under no provocation will go take a ----

I have been interested in 'smelly old shacks' or privies since my boyhood, because my first 11 years (1932–44) were accompanied

4

by a pull-and-let-go water closet in a brick outhouse next to the coalhouse 'up the yard', or up the garden. I remember how draughty and cold it could be in bad weather spending the proverbial penny, making it a very moving experience, and chamberpots or guzunders were still the order of the night. I also remember the tin bath hanging on the wall of our lavatory in which we all took our weekly bath, one at a time, in front of the sitting room fire on a Friday or Saturday night. Then, in 1944, our lives were transformed when we moved to a house with an indoor lavatory and bathroom, as exciting an event in my memory as the news of the D-Day invasion which happened about the same time.

The great majority of people in Britain also enjoyed this momentous sea-change from outdoor to indoor loos between the 1930s and the 1960s. Talking to so many people in their 60s, 70s and 80s, to gather material for this book, has revealed to me how many people in Worcestershire regard this move from draughty seats in old shacks to indoor seats placed cosily on high, next to their bedrooms, as the greatest single material improvement in their lives. It is easy to forget that most people in this country had outside lavatories before the Second World War and that many of these were shared between a number of families. By the 1960s most households in Britain had at least one indoor loo and by the 1990s most 'executive' style houses had three or four. I now live in a house built in 1975 with three toilets and cardboard-thin indoor walls. When our four teenage daughters lived with us there seemed to be fairly continuous flushing of the said loos, with noisy cascades of water heard throughout the house. I realised then that I had lived through the siphonic revolution of the 20th century – and I often found myself looking back with nostalgia at those quiet times in that old outdoor shack of my childhood.

ALAN RICHARDS

5

The author outside his first great find – an intact wooden privy in Stoke Priors (see also chapter 4) – belonging to Bernard and Olive Poultney.

[1]

THE DARK INSANITARY AGES

The Romans loved their loos and they began the first sanitary revolution 2,000 years ago in England, when they brought their lavatories, flushed by water, northwards to Worcestershire, and even as far north as the very draughty Hadrian's Wall where the remains of their communal military loos can be seen at forts like Housesteads. The Picts and the Scots beyond the Wall sadly did not receive this great boon and blessing bestowed by the Romans on the English. Southern travellers like Dr Samuel Johnson and Tobias Smollett were still complaining about the lack of privies in Scotland 1,800 years after Julius Caesar first arrived on the Kentish coast. Dr Johnson summed up Scotland's sanitary provision: 'The Scots take good care of one end of a man but not the other.'

The Romans built a fort at Droitwich to protect Worcestershire's very valuable salt industry. It was laid out to a standard plan, complete with a communal latrine like the one at Housesteads, where soldiers sat on a single wooden bench seat around three walls facing each other convivially, brandishing their bum sponges on the end of sticks. The wooden seat was pierced with about 20 holes and was built over a trench trough through which diverted river water ran continuously. The sponges were rinsed in a narrow channel of water at the feet of the sitters. In Droitwich the Romans may have rinsed them more hygienically in salt water.

When the Roman army left Britain in AD 411, with the subsequent collapse of Roman rule and of their flushing lavatories and elaborate sewers, the Britons slipped back into their old native ways of sewage disposal, namely, squatting down in the

Roman military latrine at Housesteads fort on Hadrian's Wall. (Painting by Ronald Embleton)

fields and woods around their dwellings. Nothing like the loos and sewers of the Romans was seen again in Britain for the next fourteen centuries. This long period of squatting and squirting in the fields or in the nearest dark corner lasted until the twilight years of Queen Victoria, whose beloved Prince Albert was struck down by typhoid in 1861.

The Vikings raided Worcester, sailing up the river Severn many times between AD 800 and 1000. A Viking outside lavatory was found during excavations on the site of Viking York (Yorvic), and it has been reconstructed in the Viking Centre. It was the state of the art system before the Normans arrived and started to build stone castles and draughty castle privies. This Viking loo consisted of a hole in the ground, surrounded by a low wattle fence, with pieces of animal skins replacing the

A Viking and his loo at the Viking Centre in York. For this relief much thanks.

Roman sponges on sticks. The look of bliss on the reconstructed Viking's face, as he squats over the hole, may show his appreciation of the soft and luxurious pre-Andrex bottom wipers which are hanging from the top of the fence, no doubt cut carefully into squares.

There was a short sanitary step forward after 1066, at least for our Norman conquerors, who built in their castles very lofty stone privies which they called garderobes. The privy outlets jutted out from castle towers with a long drop for the sewage, straight into the moats where goldfish thrived on the droppings of Norman aristocrats. Worcester Castle must have had several of these garderobes but only the castle mound now survives. Holt Castle, further upstream on the Severn, still has its 14th-century sandstone tower, which also must have contained garderobes, or 'withdraughts' as they were more truthfully called. Garderobe is the French for wardrobe and is an early example of the scores of euphemisms used for the house of easement. Some of the castle privies were high-up two or three-holers with wider projections than single-holers, making them even draughtier and more vulnerable to daring besiegers, who sometimes crawled up these sewage outlets or stone chutes to take the sitting defenders by – a very nasty – surprise.

Many abbeys and priories had piped water before AD 1200, and monks were probably the first to build toilets with flushing water in Worcestershire after the Romans had left. The remains of the privies of Worcester Priory can be seen on the west side of the cathedral and were built on the bank of the Severn so that the sewage would be flushed down into the river. The latrine block was called the reredorter and was usually in the wing next to the dormitory. There were rows of seats because of the strict monastic timetable, which meant that even movements of the monks' bowels were regulated by the tinkling of the bells.

The long-drop castle privies were adopted and refined by the

A very draughty garderobe at Castle Stalker in Scotland, with a drop of 100 feet down the castle wall.

builders of manor houses in the 15th and 16th centuries. Stone and brick channels were built from the bases of indoor privies, which hid the passage of the sewage from view and avoided the tell-tale brown stains on the walls underneath the older projecting garderobes. Harvington Hall, near Chaddesley Corbett, has a very good example of a brick channel from a privy on the first floor by which the sewage was taken straight down into the moat, which is still teeming with goldfish.

By the 16th century the houses of the gentry and nobility had indoor and outdoor privies but these were not flushed by running water. The most picturesque outdoor privy in Worcestershire is in the grounds of Huddington Court, near Droitwich, which is one of the loveliest timber-framed houses in Britain. This is an early example of an earth closet, complete with a lat-

Harvington Hall – waste from the privy with the small window fell straight down the brick shaft into the moat.

A Tudor privy in the garden of Huddington Court – the loveliest loo in the county.

ticed window. Guy Fawkes himself may have used this privy because many of the Gunpowder Plotters held secret meetings in this home of the Wintour family, and the three Wintour brothers lost their lives as a result of the plot in 1605.

Super Statuto que nul ject dung

This is one of the earliest public health acts, passed during the reign of Richard II – a writ that no-one is to dump dung. Shortly after his splendid attempt to clean up England, he was deposed, and the indiscriminate dumpers of dung no doubt rejoiced.

[2]

SMALL CORNERS

Worcestershire was an important arsenal for both Royalists and Roundheads during the Civil War of the 17th century with the manufacture of cannon, swords, muskets and gunpowder. The key ingredient in the making of gunpowder is saltpetre (potassium nitrate), which was collected by saltpetre men, and they had the right to dig wherever the earth had been soaked with urine or dung for saltpetre. In 1607 all the saltpetre men were put under the charge of the Earl of Worcester and they dug in the pits of privies (earth closets), in stables, dovecotes, cellars, cattleyards, pigeon lofts, sheepfolds and even under the pews of some Worcestershire churches. These invasions of private property and of privies for 'privy earth' brought many complaints, and in 1628 the saltpetre men justified their digging in churches in one of their reports: 'The women piss in their seats, which causes excellent saltpetre.' Sermons were of course much longer then and so were women's dresses, and there were no public toilets for women until after the First World War.

The county was also a centre for cloth-making until the 19th century and human urine was collected and sold for use in the manufacture of woollen cloth in towns like Worcester, Bromsgrove and Kidderminster. Tanning was another important industry in Bromsgrove where hides were prepared by using warmed hen, dove and dog dung. The stink was so bad from the tanneries that tanners could only prepare hides during certain sixteen and eight day periods.

Many of the mansions of the Catholic nobility and gentry in Worcestershire had indoor privies which sometimes disguised

14

entrances into hiding places for priests (priest holes) during the reigns of Elizabeth I and James I. These privies were usually located in closets or cupboards next to fireplaces or chimney breasts. The sound structures of the large chimney flues enabled builders to include shafts from the privies, down which the sewage dropped into cesspits in cellars or into moats. The Catholic owners of great houses like Grafton Manor, Harvington Hall, Huddington Court, Hindlip Hall, Hadzor Court and Hewell Grange all had priest holes, many of them built by the expert craftsman Nicholas Owen. The best surviving examples of his work are to be seen at Harvington Hall where one of the priest holes is reached through a privy on the second floor from where a fugitive priest could descend a narrow ladder into a very cramped hiding place.

Hindlip Hall near Droitwich had even more priest holes than Harvington Hall. It had 36 rooms and a bewildering labyrinth of passages and halls. According to people who knew the house before its demolition in the early 19th century, every room, including its privies, had 'a trap door, a recess, a passage or secret stairs; several chimneys had double flues, one for smoke and one a priest hole.' After the arrest of the Gunpowder Plotters in 1605, Hindlip Hall was searched for two priests who were known to be hiding there and it took a posse of searchers eleven days to find them. The priests were in a filthy state and were starving after so long in a very confined space. Their first request was to be led to 'a house of office' (a privy), where they found some of the floorboards had been taken up. The searchers had expected the priests to try to use the privy under cover of night and in the words of Father Garnet, one of the priests, 'I found boards taken up, where there was a great downfall, that one should have broken his neck, if he had come thither in the dark; which seemed intended on purpose.'

Chimneys in these great houses could be very deceptive as the

Grafton Manor – the false chimney is on the left. Sewage ran down the shaft to the stone-framed outlet at its base.

owners of Grafton Manor, near Bromsgrove, found less than ten years ago. They discovered that one of the many chimneys was a false one and that it was built as a privy shaft. There is still a bricked-up stone-framed hatch in the brick base of the chimney from which the sewage could be emptied.

[3]

CHAMBERPOTS AND SLOP PAILS

Worcestershire was at the centre of a revolution in the manufacture of chamberpots in the middle of the 18th century. Potters in Worcestershire and Staffordshire perfected the art of making china white throughout its thickness and firms like the Royal Worcester Porcelain Company began to make beautiful jerries (the common name for pots since the 14th century) in large quantities. Never have so many people poured so much effort into one Worcestershire receptacle. The copying of imported Chinese and Japanese pottery was all the rage in the 18th century and Dr John Wall of Worcester was one of several inventors who experimented in producing soft soapstone paste china and his factory was making fine white porcelain by 1754. The fine white ware of the potters made a good base for coloured glazes and the Royal Worcester Porcelain Company was one of the pioneers of transfer-printing patterns in china. The jerry thus decorated now became a thing of beauty and available to many more people because of this quick and cheaper method of decoration. China chamberpots – smooth, impervious, durable and non-corrodible – had many advantages over those of earlier times made of materials that were not easy to clean, including unglazed earthenware, pewter, tin, copper and, for the lucky few, silver and gold.

The Royal Worcester Porcelain Company has produced great quantities of chamberpots yet its museum has only three examples, one of them being a large, stately jerry with two handles, made as part of a special order for a wealthy customer. Even more surprising is the omission of any reference to chamberpots in the histories of the firm, which suggests that there has been an

17

Olive and Bernard Poultney of Stoke Prior with items from their marvellous collection. The bourdaloue on the left was shaped like a slipper for ladies' use.

attempt to wipe out the memory of the production of these most necessary yet embarrassing articles. Worcester does not take the same pride in its great contribution to the beautifying of the ubiquitous jerry as the North Staffordshire potteries, with their superb lavatorial section in the Gladstone Pottery Museum, Stoke-on-Trent.

A Victorian chamberpot and bourdaloue (right) in the Royal Worcester Porcelain Company Museum. (Photo courtesy of the Curator)

Wealthier people began to use close-stools in the Middle Ages, which were just pots in boxes with a hole in the top. The removable container inside the close-stool was also often a bucket. By the 18th century the close-stool was made in the form of a bed-side table and the pot was kept in its cupboard or drawer. It was then called a night commode and many of these were still being used well into the 20th century. One of my grandmother's most

19

treasured possessions was a commode with three steps, each countersunk with a piece of carpet, and it was used to ascend into a high feather bed.

Both chamberpots and close-stools were considered so valuable that they were left fairly often by Worcestershire people in their wills, and were sometimes listed in probate inventories. Most of the bequeathed jerries were made of pewter up to the 18th century. In 1668, for example, Roger Blick, a Bromsgrove innkeeper, left a close-stool and a pewter pan in his will, and in 1683 Robert Harvey, a yeoman/glover of Bromsgrove, left a close-stool chair and a pewter chamberpot. In a 1725 inventory, a close stool was valued at 2 shillings, but another inventory in 1724 valued a close-stool and pan at 7/6d. Eleven chamberpots belonging to the Crown Inn in Bromsgrove were included in an inventory of 1679.

One of the exhibits in the museum of the Royal Worcester Porcelain Company is a large, tall white vase with a delicate gold band around its rim. This was a night or slop jar into which the contents of chamberpots were emptied each morning by the servants in the great houses. In more humble households, buckets or slop pails were used. In the book, *Worcestershire Within Living Memory*, a lady recalled her early life in a rambling old house in the 1920s and highlighted the importance of slop pails and the absolute necessity of chamberpots in the majority of houses which still did not have bathrooms and indoor loos: 'Every morning, whoever went to "do upstairs", took with them a slop pail, a slop cloth, a large jug of water and probably a mop. This of course because bedmaking included emptying the water that had been used for washing, and also emptying and washing the chamberpots. Slop pails had lids with a slope towards the centre where there was a hole, protected by a raised knob which enabled liquid to be poured in without lifting the lid. In these days of indoor sanitation, it is difficult to realise

China night or slop jar – for the contents of chamberpots – in the Royal Worcester Porcelain Company Museum. (Photo courtesy of the Curator)

the primitive conditions that prevailed, and the great need of chamberpots. Most people had to rely on a privy midden, which was a hole in the ground with a seat over containing one, two or even three holes. For obvious reasons was situated as far from the house as possible. Torches with batteries had not yet arrived, a lantern was not always available and candles easily blew out, so after dark the chamberpot was a necessity.'

An account of life in Hollydene Cottage in Stoke Prior in the 1920s by a member of the Honeybourne family, who had lived in the three-bedroomed cottage since 1835, stressed the fertilising role of jerries and slop pails: 'In each of the three bedrooms was a washstand with a marble top. This held a large jug and basin with matching soap dish, a toothbrush container, a carafe of water and glass and in a cupboard underneath were two chamberpots. A towel rail was attached at either end of the washstand. Each morning chamberpots were emptied into a slop pail, the contents diluted with water and given to the kidney beans!

'An earth closet outside had two seats, one low down for the children, the other raised up ... The closet was limed, the contents emptied once a year and used as garden fertiliser.'

The emptying of chamberpots was still a daily chore in many Worcestershire inns until the 1950s and 1960s. Ma Hood and her three daughters, Dolly, Edna and Chris, ran the Royal Oak at Broadwas in the 1930s and the following extract is part of a graphic account of life in that inn to be found in *Worcestershire Within Living Memory*: 'Breakfast over, the day's work began, sweeping out the bar and taproom, fresh sawdust on the floor, wash and disinfect spittoons, polish table and brass, wash ashtrays. Edna replenished stocks, checked the till, ordered new supplies. Ma presided over the kitchen preparing the midday meal, cutting thick sandwiches for the bar. Dolly and Chris rushed upstairs doing the bedrooms, emptying the slops, washing chamberpots, jugs and basins, making beds and doing their best to get rid of the grey stuff that accumulated under the beds. There was much flicking of dust out of the windows.'

[4]

PRIVIES AND PIGSTIES

Pit privies were widespread in the county in the second half of the 18th century. These were pit and plank jobs in their most basic form with some sort of building over them. Only the comparatively well off had brick-built privies at first and the majority were wooden. Digging the hole for a pit privy was the fundamental step and it was vital to get this right. In the words of Lem Putt, an American privy builder, in that classic little gem *The Specialist* by Charles Sale: 'Now about the diggin' of her. You can't be too careful about that,' I sez; 'dig her deep and dig her wide. It's a mighty sight better to have a little privy over a big hole than a big privy over a little hole. Another thing; when you dig her deep you've got 'er dug; and you ain't got that disconcertin' thought stealin' over you that sooner or later you'll have to dig again.'

Pit privies held sway until the late 19th century when they began to give way to bucket privies. In many of the villages of Worcestershire there was no piped water supply until the 1960s and buckets were still being used in rural areas until a better supply of running water made the installation of water closets possible. The first wooden privy that I was invited to inspect belongs to Bernard Poultney and his wife Olive at Sharpway Gate in Stoke Prior. It turned out to be a real beauty in a secluded position in their 2 acre garden on the edge of Hanbury Woods. It was built with a tiled roof in 1920 as the outdoor privy of a matching wooden bungalow, and was a one-holer with a bucket underneath which was emptied by lifting the elm seat of the thunder-box. There are several very distinctive features of this privy which makes it worthy of a conservation order. One

The one-hole tollhouse privy – with trapdoor for emptying – now at the Avoncroft Museum. (Photo courtesy of the Director, Dr Simon Penn)

Picturesque wooden privy, complete with hurricane lamp, belonging to Olive and Bernard Poultney.

side is decorated with large horseshoes and chains which were once used to fasten timber on horse-drawn carts. The interior is lofty, cosy and draughtproof with a large window overlooking an old orchard. Its floor has an inlaid pebble mosaic, the work of George Stanton of Hanbury. It would be a very fine acquisition for the Avoncroft Museum of Buildings just 3 miles away.

In contrast the Avoncroft Museum has the stateliest brick-

Bernard Poultney inside his wooden privy, sitting on the elm seat beside the large window with its orchard view.

built privy in the county – a three-holer, with two holes for adults and a smaller hole for children. It was rescued from the garden of a great house near Leominster, where it was built over a very deep cesspit emptied through a large trapdoor in the floor in front of the seats. This dignified privy has some fine decorative panelling in the wall facing the seats and sash windows, giving the sitters a delightful view of the garden.

Max Harper enjoying the spacious comfort of the middle seat in the splendid 18th-century three-hole privy at the Avoncroft Museum. (Photo courtesy of the Director, Dr Simon Penn)

The other privy which has been rebuilt at Avoncroft is a more humble one-holer inside a wooden shed and belonged to the picturesque rural tollhouse. Like Lem Putt's wooden privy in *The Specialist* it faces east and gets the full benefit of the morning sun. Its wooden door swinging in and its position on a grassy knoll brings back Lem Putt's description of the therapeutic

The author inspecting the tollhouse privy at the Avoncroft Museum. His daughter, Virginia Richards, is investigating the adjacent woodshed. (Photo courtesy of the Director, Dr Simon Penn)

effects of sitting on his carefully designed privy: 'So I built his door like all my doors swingin' in, and, of course, facing east, to get the full benefit of th' sun. And I tell you, gentlemen, there ain't nothin' more restful than to get out there in the mornin', comfortably seated, with th' door about three-fourths open. The old sun beatin' in on you, sort of relaxes a body – makes you feel m-i-g-h-t-y, m-i-g-h-t-y r-e-s-t-f-u-l.'

Privies were often built next door to pigsties in Worcestershire and this proximity of two smelly but very necessary buildings seems to be still common in many countries, especially in the Far East. Joe Hunt, the President of the Romsley Historical Society, was born in 1913 at the one-time Fox Hunt pub perched on Romsley Hill: 'Its range of outbuildings consisted of two pigsties, a privy and a urinal and a dung heap. The privy (a one-holer) was the end building and one's attendance there was ever punctuated by the not inappropriate grunt of the pigs. Behind the privy was a lean-to receptacle with a sloping and removable wooden roof, into which slid, from the privy, what became the night soil. Inside the privy, hanging from string, were neatly torn pieces of newsprint and many hundreds of issues of *Aris's Birmingham Gazette* neatly folded. Providing these were among my regular daily chores, along with salt grinding and knife cleaning!'

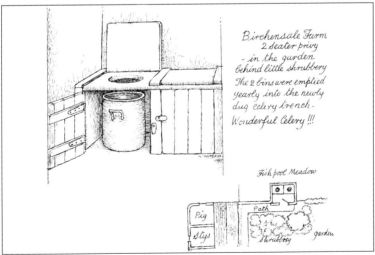

The two-hole garden privy (buckets) just round the corner from the pigsties at Birchensale Farm. (Courtesy of Norman Neasom).

A lady in Stoke Prior told me that when she was a child in the 1930s the brick-built privy for her family, too, was next to the pigsty. It was a two-holer and she and her sister used to sit on it together, because boys used to go behind the privy to make grunting noises in order to start the pigs grunting. Many of the garden privies in Cookley (near Kinver) were next to pigsties until the 1940s, and a few lucky families had two-holers. A lady in the village of Peopleton recalled living in a row of three terraced cottages in the 1940s, with one privy serving the three families and this was next to the pigsty and opposite the chickens. Several of the bungalows in Dodford, built for the Chartists in 1848, also had privies next to pigsties. Bernard Poultney, who has lived and worked on farms in Hanbury and Stoke Prior all of his life, confirmed that many of the outdoor privies there were next door to pigsties or to cowsheds.

The proximity of privies, pigsties and dung hills and their drainage into rivers and streams is well illustrated in a conveyance of 1802 of an important timber-framed property in the market town of Bromsgrove. A succession of maltsters, bakers, mercers, drapers, grocers and ironmongers occupied this building from Elizabethan times up to its demolition in the 1950s. It occupied a prime site in the ancient market place, with the river Spadesbourne as its rear boundary. The conveyance included: 'All the Pigsties and the Mixen or Dunghill Place next adjoining the brook. And all that joint use of the Pump, Necessary House and Yard.'

There was an embarrassing scandal at Bromsgrove's Public School in the 1860s (it was then called King Edward VI's Grammar School), which involved ashpits where the contents of the school's earth closets were tipped, and the use of a classroom next to the stables and piles of horse manure. When Sir Thomas Cookes of Bentley had re-endowed the small school in 1693, he

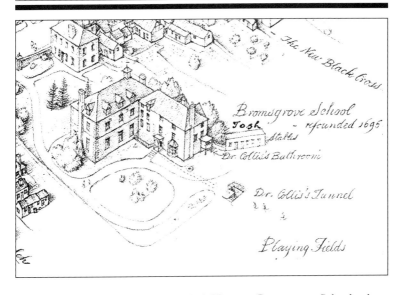

The New Black Cross.

Bromsgrove School
Tosh — refounded 1695
Stables
Dr. Collis's Bathroom

Dr. Collis's Tunnel

Playing Fields

Norman Neasom has sketched the Tosh House at Bromsgrove School, where
the poor boys were taught next to the stables.

stipulated that twelve poor boys of Bromsgrove should be edu-
cated and clothed free of charge at the school. The Bluecoat
boys were a distinctive sight in the town with their special uni-
form of a long, thick-skirted blue coat, leather belt and gaiters
and a mushroom-shaped hat. Their classroom next to the stables
was called 'Tosh House' by the other boys because it also
doubled as a washroom and the seats in it were usually awash
with water from the jugs and basins. Dr T. S. Fletcher led a campaign to improve the lot of the Bluecoat boys and he complained
strongly to the headmaster, Dr Collis, about the dirty play-
ground allocated for their use, strictly segregated from the boys
of wealthier families. This was a yard where the contents of the
privies and chamberpots were emptied in holes covered with the
ashes from the school's fireplaces. The headmaster (a Doctor of

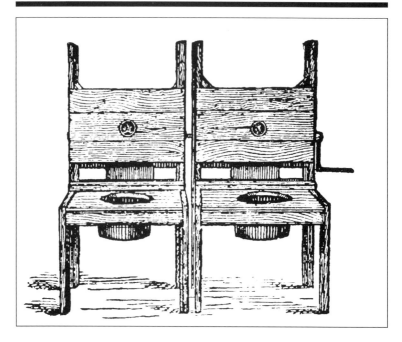

School privies designed by W. Liddiard – a multi-seater earth closet.

Divinity) told Dr Fletcher that he was satisfied with these arrangements 'considering the class of boys they are'. He seemed to believe that the combination of horse dung next to their classroom and human dung under their feet in their play-ground was a sufficiently rich environment for them. Dr Collis himself enjoyed a splendid suspended bathroom on stilts, reveal-ing some sense of hygiene, at least for his own family. The earth closets used by the boys of the school were probably on the lines of W. Liddiard's design for schools by the 1860s. He proposed a multi-seater earth closet in which a row of seats was bolted together and ashes or earth were released from the hoppers behind by means of a handle in order to cover the waste matter in the buckets below. A long wire could be fitted instead of a handle to stop children playing with the mechanism.

The rooting of pigs in the churchyard of the old parish church of Upton-upon-Severn (only the tower remains) was a constant cause of complaints by churchwardens in the 1740s. The occupants of houses neighbouring the churchyard were tipping their ashes mixed with the contents of chamberpots and privies amongst the graves, stimulating the rooting of the pigs. According to the churchwardens: 'William Pomfry and John Willoughby lay their ash heaps, hang out their old stockings and other rags in the Churchyard.'

The appetite of pigs for human excrement is harnessed in many poor countries where pigs act as sanitary agents, collecting all the available faeces. In South India some privies are built over the pigs' troughs, and all human droppings land in the troughs to the eager snuffling and grunting of the pigs. The simplest loo in China is a plank with a hole and the sitter squats over the hole above the pig trough. Pigs not only grunt loudly when welcoming offerings, but will jump up and snap at the source of food overhead. In the Hmong villages of western Thailand villagers squat among the bushy scrub and the local pigs, knowing their morning routine of emptying bowels, pursue them to their chosen squatting places with a fanfare of gleeful grunts. Few villagers appear to suffer from constipation as any delay brings immediate encirclement by hungry and expectant pigs.

[5]

SHARED PRIVIES, FOUL PRIVIES
AND ABOMINATIONS

Shared outside lavatories, whether pit privies, bucket privies or eventually the new flushed water closets, were a very common experience for many Worcestershire people before the Second World War. Even in showplace villages like Broadway, one privy shared between three houses was not unusual. One Broadway lady has recalled: 'My house in the 1920s and 1930s was a cottage in Broadway village street. There was no gas, electricity or water laid on. The toilet was shared between three cottages. It was at the end of the garden and was a long, box-like arrangement with three holes, one small one for a child and two larger ones for the adults. Next to it was the wash house an old stone sink with a tap, and a copper for boiling the washing. This too was shared by the three cottages.'

The dreaded plague, cholera, spread southwards from Scotland in 1849, and Dr T. S. Fletcher reported the first case in the Bromsgrove district at Stoke Heath in July 1849, blaming the insanitary state of the cottages there for the rapid spread of the disease. He described 'five gubbing holes of putrid, stinking water behind five cottages and one privy for five families, and one pump, the water of which was affected by a large cesspool near to the well.' He also described other cottages in Stoke Heath where 'pigsties, cesspool, noxious drains and privies were crowded behind them and close to the water wells.'

A few weeks later, in July 1849, Dr Fletcher reported that cholera had spread to the centre of Bromsgrove, after he was called to the homes of two boys, who lived in courtyards off Holy Lane (now Church Street), just round the corner from his surgery.

A shared privy (on the extreme left) in a Dudley nailers' yard in Victorian times. The nailer's workshop is in the centre of the picture.

Both boys died, and Dr Fletcher recorded: 'The pantry window of one boy's house, with its wire lattice which could not be closed, was immediately over the cesspool, and the bedroom windows were right over it. There was no circumstance to connect the two persons attacked, or their houses with each other, that could possibly give rise to the disease but this privy.'

Although Dr Fletcher was right in blaming foul privies for the spread of cholera, he followed the general and erroneous medical view that it was poisonous gases which transmitted the disease. It was not until 1854 that Dr John Snow proved that it was contaminated water supplies which transmitted cholera, and not poisoned air. The majority of doctors refused to believe this until some years later.

Many privies drained into the rivers and streams of Worcestershire, making them into open sewers that were very malodorous in hot summers in the towns and villages along their banks. In Bromsgrove, for example, an alarming number of privies drained into the Spadesbourne, or the brook as it was called. In Dr Fletcher's words: 'Our brook was really an open sewer, especially at the back of the High Street; throughout most of its course openly washing out and flowing under many closets.' The top end of Bromsgrove's High Street was a good deal sweeter than the bottom end, downstream (the Worcester Road area).

Life remained almost as insanitary in parts of Bromsgrove well into the 20th century. Charles Berwick, a railwayman all his working life, lived in the railway village of Aston Fields in the 1930s in a row of thirteen Victorian houses called Station Terrace, where all the occupants were tenants of the LMS railway company. There were nine outside lavatories for the thirteen families (over 65 people). Five of these families, for example, shared three of these very draughty loos and each family had to keep to the one assigned to their house by the LMS. He recalls unreliable cisterns which often provided such feeble flushes that it was advisable to take a bucket of water to help the flow. The lavatories were originally built as earth closets but had been converted to these very primitive water closets. The strong draughts over and under the doors caused the pipes to freeze up very easily in winter.

As Charles Berwick related: 'If your lavatory was being used and all the others in the row were empty you had to wait. Each lavatory had a wooden door with a gap of 9 inches at the top and bottom and no lights. You would often see people with a lighted candle trying to keep the flame alight during the 50 yards trek from the houses to the lavatories. We always took the *Daily Express* with us because it was the largest on offer for a penny, and it cut up into more squares which were hung on the back of the door. Sometimes people stopped on that long trek to the place of easement to collect a bucket of water to flush it. For the first fourteen years of my life I thought Jeyes Fluid was what other people called fresh air. There were no lift-up seats in our railway company's comfort stations but there was some hard material around the rims of the china pans which could be scrubbed. No-one ever got locked in ... you were not allowed to put bolts on the doors – BY ORDER OF THE LMS COMPANY!'

It was doubly unfortunate that this row of houses also shared just two outside taps with a push button to operate them, and that they also shared a large dust hole for all kinds of rubbish at the back of their lavatories. Station Terrace became known by a much more appropriate name in the mid-1930s – Bug Row – when eighteen children contracted scarlet fever during one 24 hour period, and sixteen children developed diphtheria the following year.

There were even fewer privies in parts of Sidemoor, another area of Bromsgrove. Miss E. Byng lived in a row of six houses there in the 1930s with only two privies for over 40 people. There were ten adults and children in her family and eleven in her aunt's house next door. She wrote: 'In the summertime we had to sit with our back doors open, to make a dash for the privy when it was free.'

Shared privies and dung hills proliferated in the rapidly growing cities of the 19th century and Worcester was no exception. Many houses in the crowded courts had no privies, and it was common to find a dozen families or more sharing just one. The space in the centre of many courts was used as a dung hill or midden, or more plainly as a bog, where the contents of privies and chamberpots were emptied. These bogs were regarded as valuable assets and were sold to farmers when enough ordure had accumulated over months or even years.

The first report of the Worcester Board of Health in 1832 stated: 'So far as the middens and dirt heaps are concerned, it is impossible to find words to describe their offensive state. Particularly offensive is the bog-hole in St Andrew's Square, and also the state of Farling's Entry in the Shambles, where manure and filth of all description remains till it is perfectly alive.' By the time of the second report in 1846, conditions had become even worse, but it took several outbreaks of cholera before a start was made in the 1870s on basic sanitary reforms.

Worcester's first sewage works were built in Diglis in the 1870s but these soon proved to be inadequate for the growing population. In 1903 work began on a new sewage works across the other side of the Severn; this included a tunnel under the river to carry the sewage and a very large hole was dug at Bromwich Lane in Lower Wick to receive and treat it. In the same year another deep hole was begun, this time in Upton-on-Severn, for a new sewage works in Cut Throat Lane. This small town had also suffered badly from outbreaks of cholera and many of the victims had been buried, ironically enough, in Parson's Field along Cut Throat Lane. Dung hills and other rubbish were left in the town's narrow alleys, some of which had open ditches carrying sewage and water down to the banks of the Severn. These alleys, like Lapstone Alley Dunn's Lane and New Street, were also prone to very bad flooding, when sewage flowed through the densely packed houses.

The city of Worcester became an enlightened sanitary pioneer in 1915 when it built the first public lavatories in the county for women, on land off Little Angel Street. The leading part taken by the Brotherhood and Sisterhood of Worcester, based at the Angel Street Congregational Church, in the campaign increased the odour of sanctity around this new comfort station. For this relief the ladies of Worcester must have given much thanks, though the convenience was naturally not available on the Sab-

Scores of men were employed by J. & A. Brazier Ltd between 1903 and 1906
to build the new sewage works in Worcester.

bath Day. Lavatories for women were generally regarded as
indecent and remained very rare before the First World War.
Bernard Shaw, who campaigned for more women's toilets in
the London borough of St Pancras, reported the opposition he
encountered: 'A lavatory for women was described as an abom-
ination.'

Towns and villages in Worcestershire began to build public
lavatories for men, mainly cast-iron urinals, in the 1880s and
1890s, following the Public Health Act of 1875. There is a good
example of one of these on the old GWR station in Bewdley,
which is now part of the Severn Valley Railway. In contrast,
Bewdley these days also boasts a state of the art super loo, or an
Automatic Public Convenience (an APC).

The smelliest public convenience in Bromsgrove in the 1930s and 40s. Cast-iron urinal, with lamppost on top, (right of picture) sited over the river Spadesbourne, which flows under the street at this point.

Many of the Victorian public lavatories in Worcestershire were built on the banks of rivers and streams and discharged straight into them. Before 1914 in Bromsgrove, for example, there were two public urinals, one at the top of the High Street and one at the bottom, and both were built on the banks of the river Spadesbourne, increasing its sluggish flow in dry summers (The Town Council, of course, consisted of men only and saw no need to cater for the convenience of women). The first was a smelly, cast-iron landmark in St John's Street, opposite the former Council House. According to the late Tim Brotherton, the well-known estate agent in the area for 60 years, whenever people asked for directions for the new Council House during the Second World War, they were told to follow the footpath

40

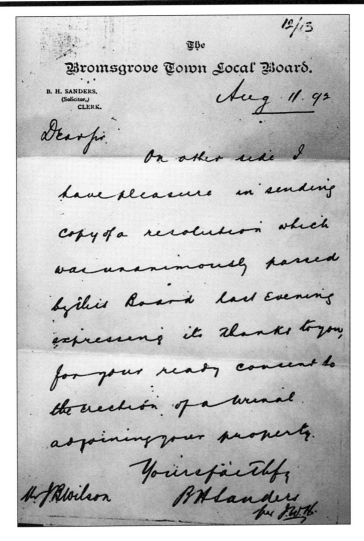

Letter dated 11th August 1892 from the Bromsgrove Town Clerk to a local grocer, J. B. Wilson, thanking him for his ready consent to the erection of a urinal next to his shop.

from Woolworths and when they came to a nasty smell they were nearly there! Others put it more briefly and said, 'Follow the pong!' When this urinal was demolished in about 1970, its smell still lingered for some weeks around the place where it had stood, the nearest thing to a loo with a ghostly presence after its demise.

The location of public lavatories was a matter of delicate negotiations between town councils and the owners of shops and other premises, who were worried about the smell and associated nuisance. In 1892, however, one noble and public spirited grocer and feed merchant in Bromsgrove, J. B. Wilson, graciously consented to the erection of a gents' urinal next to his shop at the top of the High Street. Bromsgrove Town Local Board passed a warm and glowing vote of thanks to him – in the opinion of many councillors, he deserved to be knighted for allowing it to be built next door to his shop in the most convenient position, right over the river Spadesbourne for a rapid discharge and dispersal downstream.

[6]

DEEP IN THE THUNDER-BOX SOMETHING STIRRED

In our age of well-lit indoor loos it is difficult to imagine the hazards of sitting on the seat of a garden privy in the dark while hearing the scufflings of unknown animals in the depths of the pit or bucket below. There is an abundance of stories from privy sitters about being terrified by the sounds and sudden appearances of rats, snakes, dogs, cats, cockerels, foxes, sheep, wood-lice, ferrets, mice and enormous spiders from the deep recesses of thunder-boxes.

Bernard Poultney told me about his mother's nightmarish encounter with a ferret in the two-holer privy in the garden of Normansell Farm in Lower Bentley. As she sat down on one of the holes, a little head popped out of the other hole next to her. Her family surmised later that someone had been rabbiting in the locality and had lost his ferret.

Mrs White of Redditch told me of her granny's encounter with a snake in her cottage privy in Hanbury. She was emptying a chamberpot in the privy, which was a two-holer at the bottom of the garden, when she saw the snake, rearing up through one of the seat holes, and hit it squarely on the head with the pot. This confirms one of the wisest sayings of Confucius: 'She who takes chamberpot to privy, lucky to hit snake on head and not break it.'

One dark and stormy night during the black-out of the last war, a young girl in Redditch had a truly terrifying experience when she sat down on what she thought was the seat of the garden privy. Mrs Heather Onions related how, when she sat down with her nether parts bared to the elements, to her horror

An isolated privy at Hollow Tree Farm, Vigo, near Blackwell. (Photo courtesy of Mr P. Gibbons)

she felt something cold, wet and soft moving under her. She leapt to her feet, letting out piercing screams, and her mother, aware of reports of German spies being parachuted into the Midlands, grabbed the poker and ran out to rescue her daughter from the hands of some filthy spy. There was no spy in the privy but there was a frightened, bedraggled, wet cat, which had been sheltering from the rain. For months afterwards, Mrs Onions added, she approached the privy very cautiously at night, feeling all the way round the seat before trusting her traumatised rear to it.

As we have seen in chapter 4, some privies were much closer to animals and other wildlife than others, and these often provided entertainment while sitting. Kathleen Buckle of Pershore recalled the privy next door to two pigsties, which her family shared with other families in a row of cottages. The privy and the pigs were under the same roof but the privy had a separate cesspit; it was a two-holer, one for adults and one for children. She and the other children in the cottages enjoyed the tuneful accompaniment of the grunting of the pigs when sitting in the privy. Further diversion was provided by close observation of the maggots in the cesspit. When the privy was not in use, the door was left open, but, when closed, you had to knock on the door and wait.

After a dispute with one of the neighbours a new form of entertainment began, when her stepfather built a rather crude bucket privy for the sole use of his family. The bucket was emptied into a hole in the garden. The door of the new privy was fashioned out of two potato sacks and privy was ensured by listening for approaching footsteps and shouting, 'I'm on the bog!' The entertainment came from using the privy as a hide from which unsuspecting passers-by could be seen and heard through the potato sacks. Kathleen Buckle ended her account: 'In the many years of my life I have used many different types of bog – cesspit, bucket, plunger, pull-and-let-go chain and the newer lower ones.' I wonder which type she would put first for sheer amusement value.

Mrs S. M. Baylis recalled having to shunt several sheep very often from the large farmhouse privy on the family farm between Astwood Bank and Feckenham when she was a child there in the 1940s. 'The privy was situated through the door in the walled garden and along a path to a brick building which backed onto a field. It housed a four-holer with a large hole in the middle, flanked by two smaller ones on either side, and a step down to a baby one. As I was one of seven children this was a convenient size. If we needed to make a visit after dark, three or four of us would go together, with the torch flickering and fading if the battery was on the blink. Very often we would encounter sheep vacating the privy as we arrived. If by any chance the paper had run out, two of us would have to volunteer to get some, taking the only torch of course, leaving the others to sit terrified in the dark until we returned.

'Later we moved to a house with two flushing loos, but nothing could replace the apprehension we used to feel on a cold, crisp moonlit night, making our way to the privy, not knowing what we would meet on the way there, and then sitting shivering amongst the spiders and woodlice, and then, when everyone was ready, the mad dash back to the house, hoping that one of us had remembered to shut the door to the garden otherwise it was full of sheep the next day.

'I had two older brothers and they would lie in wait for my father to visit the privy, and then would dash round into the field, lift the trapdoor at the rear where it was emptied, and torment him with anything they could lay their hands on. By the time my father had retrieved his trousers from round his ankles, and the belt from round his waist, my brothers were away across the field as fast as their legs would carry them.'

Mrs June Halfpenny recalled the wildlife which plagued all

outside privies when she described the large flies in the privy of Clock House Cottage in Fockbury, when her family moved there at the start of the Second World War. The presence of flies in privies made lids on seats a necessity in the best regulated establishments. She ended her letter most expressively: 'God! The Flies! Happy Days!' The start of the war brought a posse of plain clothes policemen to her privy at the back of the cottage to investigate a report of meetings of Nazi spies in that unlikely and not very salubrious place. Someone had painted two large swastikas inside the privy, and a report of a nest of spies in Fockbury had brought the police hurrying round, only to be buzzed by a nest of flies rather than spies.

Mrs Heather Fulcher of Kidderminster has a vivid memory of her grandfather's very noisy privy at the top end of his orchard. It was a delightful walk to the privy in summer through the apple, plum and cherry trees. Anyone who used the privy was instructed to pull like mad at a string, attached to old tin cans and chains tied onto a metal sheet, to scare away the birds who were eating the cherries. 'But in the winter,' she added, 'you ran like the wind because it was so dark and a long way from the house, or I would ask my father to stand on the back door step, and I would keep asking him if he was still there.'

She also described her aunt's little privy in Bewdley which she claimed had the best scrubbed seat in that town and was nearly white from all the hot water and soda used on it. Its door was kept locked in case anyone walked down the back alleyway and used it.

When Mrs Glennis Noke lived in Hallow as a child in the 1930s in a Victorian semi-detached cottage, her family shared the outside privy with their neighbours. Access to this privy was tortuous and rather public, involving walking past their neighbours' front door, going through their wash-house and then through a rear door and along a little path to the door of the

The 18th-century three-holer privy, with one lower seat for children, at the White House, Suckley. (Photo courtesy of Mr Geoffrey Howarth)

privy. A bucket of water for flushing the loo was obtained from a pump in the wash-house. The privy had a porcelain pan connected to the main sewer. Her brush with wildlife came one dark night: 'My most frightening experience was when I picked up a rolled-up hedgehog off the floor when reaching down to retrieve my woolly hat.'

She also recalled listening to the singing privy a few doors away, where her friend lived, one of nine children. Her friend's family had a much needed two-holer bucket privy to themselves, and this was back to back with a two-holer belonging to another household with many children. Two children from each family often sat back to back singing songs very happily and chatting.

Foxes were seen recently paying regular visits to the 18th-century three-holer of White House, Suckley, a Grade I listed build-

Mr Walton and his dog contemplate the former privy at Old Keeper's Cottage, Hanbury. It would have been a longish walk on a winter's night!

ing which belongs to Mr Geoffrey Howarth. The wooden seats, including a small one for children, are well preserved, complete with their hinged lids. Mr Howarth's neighbours were concerned that foxes had made their den in the thunder-box after they were seen entering by one seat hole and leaving by another, and they asked him to fasten down the lids to block their run.

Some people overcame their fear of going to the privy on dark

49

Stone-built two-hole privy at Bush Bank Cottage, Suckley. These days the rear outlet (below) is beautified with plants. (Photos courtesy of Mr J. M. Manderson)

nights by taking their dogs with them to stand guard. Mrs A. E. Harris, who lived in a cottage in Aston Fields in the 1960s, recalled: 'It was our lovely, faithful dog that used to sit with us in the privy on dark nights.' After one New Year's Eve party she set off for the privy accompanied by their dog and a torch: 'I was a bit the worse for wear and I dropped the flashlight in the bucket. My dear brother-in-law went to the rescue and managed to hook it out.' She added, 'In bad winters it was all hands to the pump and to the shovel in the mornings. The outside pump had to be thawed out before any water could be pumped, and we had to dig our way to the privy in the snow. Lovely, lovely days.' All the neighbouring half-a-dozen cottages had outside privies and pumps, despite the fact that Bromsgrove's sewage works were only a field away and the town centre was only a mile distant. They also depended on paraffin lamps and coal fires. She lived near the 'Stonehouse' which had a one-hole privy at the top of its garden and had once belonged to the prosperous miller of Bant Mill. Four other nearby cottages were well equipped with two-hole privies, one hole for adults and a lower one for children. It was not until 1964–1965 that these houses were put on mains water and sewers, and their privies converted at long last to flushing loos. All of them were demolished a few years later to make way for the Aston Fields industrial estate.

[7]

SEATS OF LEARNING

The outside loos at most schools before the 1950s are recalled as draughty and smelly black holes which discouraged any lingering. Later schools were built with inside loos which unfortunately came complete with their concomitant smells. There are several small seats of learning in Worcestershire with inside loos near the main entrance where the first impression on crossing the threshold is an unwholesome pong. In some large secondary schools, with their low modern ceilings, the aroma emanating from the inside toilets makes it very easy for new pupils to find them.

In the healthier schooldays of yore, most state schools had pit or bucket privies at a decent distance from the main school buildings. The great age of school building began in the late 1870s, after the Education Act of 1870 made elementary education compulsory, and School Boards built schools throughout Worcestershire with outside privies. The Brazier building firm constructed three schools for the Bromsgrove School Board in the late 1870s, Dodford School, Lickey End School and Meadows School. All of these were built with earth closets because none of them were on mains water and their only water supplies came from iron pumps in their playgrounds; they also had no drainage. All three schools are still used but their privies have been converted into water closets. A lady who is now in her 70s remembers her father emptying the fourteen privies at Dodford School every Saturday night with his shovel and wheelbarrow in the 1930s and 1940s. There were two rows of privies, one for boys and one for girls, with a channel under the small wooden seats which had to be emptied through trapdoors at their rear. Her father emptied his barrow straight onto the fields and orchard of Forest Farm, next door to the school. These privies were still in use until the 1950s when they were converted.

The dung from the school privies in Cleeve Prior was also used to fertilise an orchard, as Mike Edwards, who was born in the village, remembers. It was the village sexton's job each week to empty the school privies which were arranged in two rows, three in each, back to back, with a stone wall dividing the girls' row from the boys'. The privies were contained in one brick building with a tiled roof and the sexton used a long rake to empty the cesspit. He then wheeled his precious cargo away in his barrow to spread around the trees in his plum orchard. He claimed throughout the 1930s and 1940s that he grew the best plums in Cleeve Prior.

Hanbury village school has one of the most attractive privies, built in brick with a central gable and a tiled roof in 1928 and standing a few yards from the main school building. It used to contain about six bucket privies for the girls at the school. The boys had a two-seater 'tin' privy which was a corrugated iron shed with two bucket loos. For urine only, there was a channel and drain. There was a separate bucket privy for teachers, also well built in brick with a tiled roof. Bernard Poultney who attended the school in the 1940s remembers a Hanbury man cycling to the school every Saturday to empty the buckets either on his own garden, or sometimes burying the contents near the school.

Mr Oliver Barton was born in Claines and attended the St John's Church of England School there in the 1940s. He recalls that there were six privies for boys and six for girls which were separated by a gap 10 feet wide. They drained into a pit which the vicar's gardener used to shovel out once a week by wheeling his barrow through the gap. He then lined the pit with cinders from the open fires in the classrooms. The only water in the

Hanbury School girls' privies, built in 1928.

The teachers' former bucket privy at Hanbury School.

school was obtained from a big iron pump just outside the head-master's room. The villagers of Claines had to wait for their first water closets until the 1960s when mains water reached them.

The primitive privies and lack of washing facilities in rural schools are made very clear in the account of a lady who was born in Pebworth in 1898 and started to attend its village school when she was 4 years old. Her account is given in *Worcestershire Within Living Memory*. There was no water laid on at the school at all, not even an outside pump. She described 'carrying water from the wash house of a house two doors away'. As there were about 100 children at the school in 1902, ranging in age from 4 to 14 years, and only two earth closets, it is easy to imagine a continuous queue of children waiting to use them, and then forming another queue to wash their hands in the same bucket of water, or under the tap belonging to the very kind but hard pressed neighbour two doors away.

Some rural schools remained in a bad odour from when they were built in the 1870s or 1880s right up to the time they were connected to mains water and sewers There were continual complaints about the malodorous state of the outside privies at Cut-nall Green village school, near Droitwich, from the 1880s to the 1950s. One inspector wrote in 1886: 'It is impossible to stay an hour at a time in one classroom without opening all the windows. The smell is overpowering.' There were four earth closets at the rear of the school which had 162 children on its roll by 1888. The privies were too close to the school and were built on low-lying land with a high water table, which led to liquid sewage with a more powerful pong. Some dry earth closets were added later, but complaints about bad odours invading the school persisted until the first flushing loos were installed.

Pushing nettles or holly through the trap doors at the rear of some school privies to tickle vulnerable naked bottoms appears to have been a favourite prank. The privies at Harvington's village school (near Evesham) were across the schoolyard in the 1920s and the boys' closets were separated from the girls' by a wall. One lady's father, who attended the school at that time, delighted in telling the tale of 'having sneaked round the back of the girls' closets and nettled the bare bottoms of the girls sitting on the seats by reaching through the back doors at the back of the building.'

The same prank was played on a female teacher at the old Catshill village school near Bromsgrove. The privies for males and females backed onto each other and according to a lady who attended the school just before 1914 one boy took his revenge on his least favourite teacher by waiting for her to go to the privy, and then 'he found a gap just big enough to push a piece of holly through'.

[8]

THE INDOMITABLE SHOVELLERS

At least one man in North Worcestershire in the 1981 census described himself as a sanitary operative. His reply to the second question asking for details of what he actually did was clear and succinct: 'Shovelling shit'. One of the oldest euphemisms for these intrepid workers is night soil men, or nightmen, the successors of the 'gongfermors' who had the unenviable – but often well paid – job of emptying medieval cesspits. Before main sewers were built they performed one of the most vital jobs in any human society. They generally came at night to shovel out the sewage into wooden barrels or buckets which they emptied into their horse-drawn carts, often having to carry their stinking loads through houses into the street.

The muck carts, into which privy buckets were emptied, and the aroma are still vividly remembered by many people over the age of 50. Bernard Poultney recalls the Hanbury muck cart with its two large buckets, each with two handles, swinging at its rear as it wended its ponging way from privy to privy right up to the 1960s. Joe Hunt of Romsley has clear memories of the casual farmworkers who acted as part-time night soil men in the 1920s and 1930s: 'Every large Romsley farm had an outcast, a Caliban, who ate with the family but lived rough and slept usually over the stables or byre. They were well known in the village and usually had a nickname. Newtown Farm had its "Liverpool Jack", and Fallows Farm had its "Billy Drop". Invariably these men were paid no wages, dressed like scarecrows, lived off the farm produce, ate in the farm kitchen and whatever money they earned was from their part-time occupation as night soil men. Our night soil man was "Liverpool Jack" and his visits

Lesley Poultney with shituss scoop and cesspit, ensuring a good fruit crop in a Worcestershire orchard.

(at about 3 months' intervals) were quite significant events in the social round. He came by appointment with his horse and cart, which was backed up to the privy pit and the contents were shovelled into place.

'There is a story told locally how on one such visit Jack dropped his ancient jacket into the faeces pit, and when asked why he bothered to fish for such a relic, he replied: "Don't be so bloody daft. My lunch is in the pocket!"

'When the cart was filled, the contents were carted off and

Sid King, one of Bromsgrove's best-remembered night soil men, pictured with his horse and cart for the town's carnival procession in 1930. The cart had been specially fumigated so the council foreman, Mr D. Healey, was standing proudly alongside.

deposited onto one of the farm fields. "Liverpool Jack" was a staunch Methodist (of the Primitive variety) and could be seen and smelt every Sunday night at the Romsley Primitive Methodist Chapel, which is now a private residence in Dark Lane.'

Mr Oliver Barton, who was born in Claines near Worcester has a clear memory of Harry, a night soil man of the Claines and Fernhill Heath area from the 1930s to the 1960s. Harry was a regular at the Bull pub in Fernhill Heath, and the other customers were aware of his powerful presence as soon as he entered the bar, where they slowly edged away from him. Harry never seemed to cut his fingernails and they were always black underneath. The people of the area were dependent on

Harry for emptying their cesspits and buckets until the early 1960s when they were at last connected to the mains water supply and flushing lavatories were installed. Mr Barton recalls that until then water for drinking and washing was pumped up from the outdoor wells into tanks. Each pair of houses shared a well, a tank and a pump, and took it in turns to do the pumping.

The night soil men in Bromsgrove began emptying privies at midnight in the 1880s. Arthur James who lived in Norton, 1 mile to the north of Bromsgrove, recorded that the noise of horses and carts and the clanging of buckets could be heard in Norton as soon as the night soil men reached the Birmingham road. This was the signal for people to start closing their windows. There was a bad outbreak of typhoid fever there in 1887 with a fatality in almost every house in Walton Road and Barnsley Road. Arthur James had no doubts about the cause of his brother's death: 'No wonder the fever broke out. The sanitation at this time was anything but good. The water was obtained from a pump not far from the privy, which was by the way an open midden and next to the pantry.'

The stink of privies being emptied in the village of Catshill, 2 miles to the north of Bromsgrove, has been described by Mrs Nora Wheeler, now in her nineties, the daughter of the landlord of the Plough and Harrow there. The pub had three privies which were emptied every few months or so and the emptying day was 'an event which everyone in the village knew about! There were plenty of volunteers in those hard times as the payment was ten bob.' Most of the people in Catshill were nailers up to the First World War and they lived in small one-up and one-down cottages with privies at the bottoms of their gardens. The wooden seats of these one-holers were scrubbed every day and were emptied into a large hole in the garden. The first council houses were built in Catshill (in Woodrow Lane) in 1921 but they were still built with the old-style privies in their gardens.

Mrs Heather Fulcher remembers Blossom, the horse which pulled the night soil cart around Bewdley and Wribbenhall in the 1930s and 1940s. Blossom was kept in a field in Wribbenhall and she used to feed her with apples and mints over the back wall. She added, 'When Blossom was about, you did not hang about. The scent around her was usually very strong.'

Some houses within half a mile of Bromsgrove's town centre still depended on the council's night soil men until the late 1950s. A lady, who lived at Moat Mill Farm in Charford, described the old Moat Mill house as large, with twelve rooms but with no flushing toilet and no indoor sanitation of any kind all the time she and her five brothers and sisters and parents lived there, right up to 1957.

It seems to have been fairly common for sisters to use two or three-hole privies together, especially after dark. Norman Neasom recalls how in the 1930s three sisters at Hadzor Court Farm usually sat together on the three-holer privy which was next to the cider mill and some distance from Hadzor Court House. He also remembers that the sisters' Aunt Polly, who was brought up in stricter Victorian times, often voiced her concern that this was disgusting, and not how young ladies were brought up in her day.

Much of the night soil collected was spread on fields since farmers were willing to pay for the rich products of privies and of middens. When Norman Neasom's father was farming at Birchensale, he paid night soil men to deliver sewage from Redditch – and he grew very fine tomatoes and celery. The Worcester and Birmingham Canal brought a great blessing to farmers in the form of boatloads of ripe Birmingham sewage which enriched the heavy clay soil. Farmers along the canal had their own wharves where the sewage was disembarked and from where they sent their produce to Birmingham and Worcester markets.

Miss Greaves of Barnt Green, whose family has farmed at Lane House Farm, Alvechurch since Victorian times, remembers canal barges still bringing Birmingham sewage to Lane House Wharf, near Aqueduct Lane, in the 1920s and 1930s as they had done in her grandfather's time in Queen Victoria's reign. She also recalls that these humming cargoes from Birmingham included collections from cesspits and middens, as well as horse droppings from the streets. When this rich Brummie mixture had been spread on a field for some time, the reddish Worcestershire soil turned black and produced the heaviest crops of potatoes Miss Greaves has ever seen. Most of these potatoes were then transported by canal to Birmingham's markets. This is a beautiful example of the recycling of human waste. All kinds of small objects were dropped into Birmingham's privies and dung heaps and Miss Greaves recalls finding scores of pens, pencils and inkpots scattered over the fields of her family's farm. No doubt future archaeologists will deduce from finding such a density of objects on the farm that it was once the site of a large school, with some very unwilling pupils. John Burman of Alvechurch also attributes the vigour of the roses in his garden at the bottom of Aqueduct Lane to those rich cargoes.

The spreading of Brummie sewage on Tardebigge farms along the canal was one of the secrets of the sweet smell of success of the Dixons' farming business in the village. Thomas Dixon founded the business in the early 19th century and five generations of the family have continued it. The Rev Alan White, author of *The Dixons of Tardebigge*, has confirmed that the magical mixture from Birmingham had much to do with the flavour and size of the fruit and vegetables which they sent by boat to the city's markets. There was a smelly symmetry about the exchange of cargoes between Birmingham and Worcestershire: boats carried cargoes of sewage to be spread on the fields, and on their return

The author tries his hand at shovelling at a former Chartist cottage of 1848 in Dodford, now owned by the National Trust. This earth closet was in use until 1997.

journey they were often loaded with animal manure for the city's allotments. The loading and unloading of these stinking cargoes in Gas Street Basin made its name very appropriate.

The annual emptying of cesspits on the estates of the landed gentry was often a time of pranks and jokes by the estate workers who had to shovel the shit. In the 1940s, Bernard Poultney recalled, the estate workers at Hanbury Hall were pressed into wielding long-handled shovels once a year in order to empty the deep cesspit of the three-holer privy in the timber yard, which they had all helped to fill. One of the shovellers would be singled out as the victim of a joke, during which one man would apologise to him about dripping the contents of his shovel accidentally down the back of his coat, and would start to heave, as if overcome with nausea from the stench. One of their worst nightmares must have been the possibility of falling into such a deep and brimming pit, a veritable crater of doom.

Emptying a large privy bucket could be a very dangerous job, especially when the handle came off, as Mr Peter Cook of South Littleton related. He and his wife lived in one of the Victorian Silk Mills cottages in Badsey in the 1960s and had a large bucket privy made out of an old 5 gallon drum which had been cut down and a handle attached. One morning, after he had returned home very tired from a long nightshift as a driver, his wife asked him to empty the heavy and brimming bucket. 'The ground was already prepared so I picked up the bucket and carried it farther down the garden, when, all of a sudden, the handle went light. The bucket hit the ground hard, sending its contents of about 3 gallons into the air, covering me all over from head to foot in "Sweet Violets!" We did not have running hot water then nor a bath, but only an old wooden tub and water heated by a gas boiler.'

[9]

A Privy Pot-Pourri

Most Worcestershire houses up to the 1950s did not possess splendid water closets that boasted mahogany and brass fittings and had grand sounding names like Burlington and Rochester. Many Birmingham children were evacuated to Worcestershire in the Second World War and those who were used to outside flushing lavatories encountered the more primitive bucket or tin bath privies in the rural areas for the first time, sometimes with disastrous results. Bill Kings, the well-known local historian of Sidemoor in Bromsgrove, has a fascinating account of how one unlucky lad, about 11 or 12 years old, fell into a crater of doom on his first day as an evacuee from Birmingham in 1940.

This trusting youngster, suffering from stomach ache and an urgent call of nature, asked two Sidemoor brothers, lads of his own age, the whereabouts of the nearest lavatory. Mischievously they pointed to the large opening in the back of a corrugated iron privy, which was shared between several houses grouped around Tin Yard at the bottom end of Broad Street. It was a bucket and wooden seat job but, like similar privies in that wild and woolly side of the town, the bucket had been replaced by a more capacious tin bath which was emptied through the large hole at the rear. Most people in Sidemoor had no bathrooms and tin baths were used in front of the open fire. When a new tin bath was acquired the old one was often used under the seat in the privy. Anyhow, when the trusting evacuee went through the indicated opening he found, to his surprise, a rather full bath sloping towards him and he sat on the edge of it in his hurry to evacuate. His weight caused the unsavoury receptacle to tip and he fell backwards, up to his neck in Sidemoor dung.

There is a heartwarming end to this war story because the two brothers who had played this joke on the unsuspecting evacuee felt some remorse when he emerged from the tin privy, covered all over with not so sweet violets. They rushed him round to the only outside tap in Tin Yard, shared by all the houses, and they washed him down. The Brummie boy, having suffered this smelly initiation ceremony in the rough quarter of Sidemoor, shortly afterwards returned to his home in Birmingham, where he no doubt felt safer for the rest of the war.

Bill Kings recalls another outside privy which had inhibiting effects on the conjugal relations between a husband and wife who lived in a small cottage in Worms Ash, Dodford, with their two young daughters at the end of the Second World War. The couple heard the BBC wireless broadcast of Labour's landslide election victory on 26 July 1945, while their two daughters were sleeping upstairs. They were celebrating this historic event by making love in their sitting room, when their elder daughter entered the room closely followed by her sister, both on the way to their garden privy, which could only be reached by that route. Next day the frustrated father was the first to arrive at the Bromsgrove Council offices to demand to be put at the top of the list for one of the council houses, with a bathroom and an indoor flushing lavatory, which the new Labour government had promised to build throughout the country.

An unforeseen result of the Second World War for one Bromsgrove family was that they heard their outside water closet being flushed long after they had gone to bed. These were no ghostly flushings, as Mrs Shirley Brittan wrote: 'I lived in All Saints Road with my mother during the war, opposite the American Army Camp and Hospital, and we sure had trouble with those Yanks. The GIs did their courting in our entry and, of course, would use our lavvy. Quite a shock for Mom and me when the

Bill Kings, an intrepid privy investigator, finds a two-holer belonging to a nailers' cottage in Monsieurs Hall Lane, Bromsgrove. (Photo courtesy of Syd Allen)

chain would suddenly flush all on its own! Numerous complaints were made to the camp adjutant and things would improve for a while, but then we were back to the midnight flush.'

The worst features of the outside flushing toilets during the 1940s and the very bad winter of 1947 were summed up neatly by the same writer: "I used to daydream in our outside lavvy about my ideal lavatory. It would have a carpet, a light instead of a torch, which lay on the floor and always rolled, so that the light was never where you needed it, especially if I had taken a book with me. Most important of all it would have a door which fitted; ours had a gap above and below it. Goodness knows the reason why! When it snowed the snowflakes would blow in. It would also have a lock and the privacy for which I yearned. There would be no lagging of the pipes in the winter with pieces of cloth.

'When the frost took us by surprise in our outside lavatory, the fun would begin. The poker would have to be heated up in the fire and poked down the overflow. If that didn't work you held a candle under the bit of pipe you thought was frozen and finally Grand-dad had to be fetched. I have no idea what magic trick he used, but he could always get it unfrozen, except in 1947, when it seemed to be frozen for weeks. We then had to throw buckets of water down after we'd been.'

Despite these discomforts of an outside WC, Mrs Brittan had only to visit the pit privy of her great-grandparents' Victorian house to be reminded what a sanitary advance she enjoyed at home. She wrote: 'The worst toilet of all was at my great-grand-parents' house in Worcester Street. This one was out the back door and up some steps, and it always smelled. It was shared by many of the cottages and it was only to be used in dire emergencies. I was always told not to use it because "that's where people caught typhoid!" The fact that it had happened about 40 years before was beside the point.'

Mrs Brittan was able to experience the revolution in sanitary accommodation over four generations of her family. Her paternal grandparents had a garden privy which she found superior to the dreadful shared privy of her great-grandparents. She recalled: 'During the Second World War I spent much of my time with my father's parents Harold and Lucy Gower, because my father was in the RAF and my mother worked. They lived in Stourbridge Road, Bromsgrove, in an old nailers' cottage which shared a pit privy with the cottage next door whose occupant was Mr Giles. I was scared to go on my own in the dark and I was always frightened that Mr Giles would need to "go" while I was there. In summer it was easy for I would sit on the wooden seat with the deep hole below me, which I was sure came out in Australia, and sing at the top of my voice.

'The dark cold nights of winter were a different story. I would get all dressed up in my hat, gloves, scarf and pixie hat, and Granny would have to come with me. Of course I wouldn't let her in and she would have to stand outside in the cold, holding the torch, which shed little light because of the shade needed for the blackout. To reach the privy you came out of the back door, crossed the yard and down the garden path, and in summertime you walked beneath an arbour of wonderful pink rambling roses. I think now that they were planted deliberately to disguise the smell of the privy. It was kept as clean as possible by Granny and Mrs Giles, and every Monday, after the washing had been done, it would be scrubbed. When I was in my teens, I was ridiculed about telling people when I was going to the toilet, but it came from that wartime fear of falling into the deep black hole of my grandparents' privy and never being seen again. After all at that time my feet barely reached the ground.'

Charles Berwick remembers an occasion when he was a 17-year-old locomotive fireman and took a train from the rural peace of

Worcestershire into Birmingham during one of the worst night air raids on that city in the dark days of 1940, and ended up trying to force his way into a bombed outside lavatory. After leaving the loco sheds in Aston Fields, their train needed three bankers to get them up the Lickey Incline and this took 25 minutes. It took another three hours to reach the inner city because the main lines were used almost continually to move troop and ammunition trains up and down. When they arrived at Camp Hill bank, they were suddenly in the 'devil's cauldron' with the noise of anti-aircraft guns, bits of flying debris, dust, smoke and sparks and the 'Vroomp, Vroomp' of bombs dropping. One of these bombs fell onto Birmingham City's football ground, and another on the Birmingham Empire Theatre. After running this gauntlet of bombs, they left their train at its destination, Saltley loco sheds, 15 hours after leaving Bromsgrove, and set off home on foot.

Walking carefully along Duddeston Mill Road, which was full of bombed and burnt out houses with firemen still fighting the fires and the pavements full of rubble, they heard sounds from one of the mounds of debris. In the words of Charles Berwick: 'The debris revealed itself as an outside lavatory. Someone was in there. I found a metal bar lying on the floor and was able to prise open the door which had jammed, not without a tremendous effort though, which landed me, door and metal bar in a heap among the rubble. I looked up, sweating, and there, on a very old-fashioned lavatory, a board and bucket job, sat an old gentleman, shirt sleeved, peaked cap, and trousers round his ankles, who enquired, not too politely, "What the 'ell's going on?" I apologised and left – well what else could I do?'

I am also indebted to Charles Berwick for clearing up some of the fundamental sweet mysteries of life on the footplate of a steam locomotive on a long journey with few stops, when he explained how the resourceful driver and fireman could improvise a privy, either when travelling at speed or at a standstill. On

A two-hole privy belonging to a 16th-century farmhouse at Boreley, near Ombersley. (Photo courtesy of Mrs Margaret Peters)

long express runs they sometimes had to use the wide bucket allocated to each engine, or the fire shovel, in order to respond to an urgent movement of the bowels. The use of the fire shovel required some finely balanced and accurate squatting, but with the great advantage of a clean and speedy cremation. The easier method if the train was stationary was to rig up a bucket and plank job, by using one of the planks on the fireman's side of the engine which were usually pushed together to make a seat. One plank was put across the wide bucket and this was sufficient to contain any crisis of the bowels.

The apparently invisible means used by passenger trains to dispose of sewage is rather crude but effective. The toilets on trains have always discharged straight onto the ballast between the tracks. Hence the notices asking passengers not to flush the loos while the trains are at a standstill in stations; they don't want unpleasant heaps in sight and also under the noses of waiting passengers. From his long career as a railwayman, Charles Berwick believes that this method of jettisoning sewage worked because it was spread out as thinly and invisibly as possible: 'I must have walked miles and miles of track and never noticed any smelly heaps, so the dispersal must work.'

He found the sanitary arrangements at the LMS Waggon Works in Aston Fields much cruder. He recalled that in the 1940s, when they employed about 500 men, there were only two brick-built bucket privies, each with two seats and only a low partition between them, and a 12 inch gap at the top and bottom of the doors. They were designed so that lingering on the loo could be seen and discouraged. Chemicals were put into the buckets to sweeten the smell, but with little success, and no success at all on Mondays. Most of the men did heavy work and consumed more beer and meat than usual during their Sunday dinners. The resulting residue of beef, beer and sprouts, deposited on Mondays, was explosive and overpowering.

[1 0]

PULL AND LET GO

Of all the world's great revolutions, the French, American, Russian and Chinese, the siphonic flushing revolution, otherwise known as 'the pull and let go' revolution, has been the greatest boon and blessing to those it has reached. This revolution took off in Britain in the 1870s and 1880s, when the better off began to abandon their outside privies in favour of indoor flushing water closets. Most people however, had to wait until the 1930s and 1940s for their indoor WCs, while those in rural areas often had to wait until the 1960s.

Country children who were lucky enough to attend a newly-built Worcestershire school, however, saw their first flushing toilets in the 1920s and 1930s. Most 19th-century schools were of course provided with earth closets and some were still using these as late as the 1950s. One Wolverley lady remembers her schooldays in the new village school in 1927: 'The main attraction of the school was the novelty of flushing toilets. These were the first seen by many of the children, for these were still the days of the bucket privy which lasted until the 1940s.'

Mrs Shirley Brittan summed up the siphonic flushing revolution in her lifetime: 'Sometimes I now sit in my centrally heated house with two indoor flushing toilets and think of those outside privies. Never in my wildest dreams did I think I would end up in such luxury!'

Early indoor water closets did not flush well and were often not connected to well-ventilated sewers, which led to sewer gases coming into houses and to the spread of bacteria, causing enteric fever and typhoid in well-to-do households. George Jennings, a

London plumber, took out one of the first patents for an improved siphonic flush in 1854. The year 1885, however, was the annus mirabilis for the development of a much improved siphonic flushing WC, when two products were combined to make the most efficient and most decorative water closet the world had yet seen. Thomas Crapper, plumber to the royal family, perfected the overhead cistern so that wastage of water was prevented and the flushing was more certain and powerful. At the same time the pottery firm of Thomas Twyford in Stoke-on-Trent launched their revolutionary, finely moulded lavatory pan, called the Unitas. The firms of the two Thomas's got together to make veritable Rolls Royces of water closets, complete with mahogany seats and brass fittings. In addition, Sir Henry Doulton's factory, established near Dudley in 1848, was the first to manufacture glazed stoneware pipes which made more efficient sewers possible.

The Bromsgrove building firm of J. & A. Brazier Ltd became the champion sanitary specialists of Worcestershire in converting earth closets into water closets and building Victorian villas, complete with de-luxe bathrooms containing Crapper and Twyford loos. This firm's sanitary work ranged from large-scale sewage works for towns like Worcester, Redditch and Upton-on-Severn to building and cleaning cesspits, repairing water closets and unblocking drains on the stations of the Midland Railway Company between Barnt Green and Droitwich. Mrs Bolding, the wealthy owner of Boldings Brewery in Bromsgrove, was an enthusiastic converter of earth closets into water closets in her properties in the 1890s. She owned several houses in Hanover Street where she employed the Brazier firm to update the privies. In 1898 the same firm built two large Victorian villas for Mrs Bolding in New Road, which was then Bromsgrove's most fashionable suburb, and these boasted lavish bathrooms with monumental mahogany lavatory fittings.

A converted privy at Old Bell Cottage, Hanbury. Mrs Rosalind Tomlinson has preserved the seat of the former earth closet.

J. & A. Brazier also installed de-luxe loos in the Raven Hotel, Droitwich. Three state-of-the-art water closets were supplied by the firm of Henry Doulton, near Dudley, complete with mahogany seats, brass hinges and cisterns in 1913. The cost price to J. & A. Brazier of each of the glazed, fireclay lavatory pans was 10 shillings, which was less than the price of the mahogany seats at 13/4d each. The price of lavatory pans had fallen by this time, 1913, because they were being cast by using liquid clay, a faster process than the old one of building up clay on a mould by hand.

A Thomas Crapper cistern with a Thomas Twyford
pedestal, 1885.

THE COUNTRY SEAT
by Christopher Curtis

They were built like emporia in the reign of Victoria,
In the castle, or manor, or grange,
With their seats made of wood, which have gamely withstood
Pressures greater than mere winds of change.

Boys with bats, balls, or oars, sportsmen sporting 12-bores
Gaze in rows from the walls on the sitter,
Draughts and damp old stone tiles mean today's stately piles
Suffer badly from cold that is bitter.

But, forget all the strain, pull the gleaming brass chain
(With a porcelain handle, no less),
And, released by a piston, from within a vast cistern
Comes a roar – and you're flushed with success.

By the start of the 20th century the conversion of earth closets into water closets was gathering pace. In 1903 J. & A. Brazier converted the priest's garden privy into a WC at St Peter's presbytery in Rock Hill, Bromsgrove. The cost to the priest for the comfort of this modern convenience 'with water laid on' was £6 15s, which was equivalent to about seven or eight weeks' wages for most manual workers. The priest was ahead of his time in employing the same firm to convert the earth closets of St Peter's school into water closets at a cost of £49, a year's pay for most of the fathers of the children. The new loos provided these youngsters with their first experience of 'pull and let go' chains followed by cascades of water. Most of them had to wait another thirty or more years before the earth closets at their parents' homes were converted.

In 1939 many people from the Strand area of Bromsgrove transferred from their old Victorian cottages to brand new council houses in Sidemoor. Mr and Mrs X, now in their 70s, have vivid memories of their move from 'Bug Alley', as they called their yard in the Strand, where there was a row of eight outdoor bucket privies shared between sixteen families, each privy with a stable style of door. These cottages were so insanitary that when their occupants were moved to their new houses, the council insisted that their furniture should be fumigated. Mr and Mrs X remember their furniture being left outside on the pavement for two days afterwards. Nevertheless they had a flushing loo and a bathroom for the first time in their lives; electric lighting instead of paraffin lamps, and three bedrooms instead of two, all for a rent of 6/8d a week. To crown this luxury they added a second loo in 1988, when they converted a coalhouse into a downstairs toilet. They still look back on 1939 as a year of marvellous change for them, despite the outbreak of the Second World War a few months after they got their first experience of the flushing revolution.

Like many stately homes, Hanbury Hall, the home of the Vernon family until the 1950s, was fitted with some early WCs but the Vernons found that you can lead some horses to water without being able to make them drink. There were over 30 male and female servants living at the Hall before the First World War. They had their own rooms in the attic, some distance from the servants' loos on the ground floor, and some of the menservants found it too irksome to wend their way downstairs at night. According to an unimpeachable source, several of these servants found a quicker way, which demanded some degree of acrobatic skill. They opened their attic windows and used the rainwater gutter just below as their pissoir, and there was keen competition to win the title of champion marksman

Hanbury Hall circa 1910, seat of the Vernon family.

by filling the gutter with a regular flow without spillage. This nightly sport came to an abrupt end when Sir Harry Vernon caught one of his servants, red-handed and red-faced, at one of the attic windows and sacked him on the spot. The gutter being used as a lofty pissoir unfortunately drained into a soft-water butt, from which Sir Harry and other members of his family drew water for washing purposes. It is not recorded how long this peculiar practice had been indulged in by sundry menservants, but it is clear that the Vernon family had been the unknowing recipients of what was considered a valuable urine therapy in India (where former Prime Minister Mr Dessi famously drank his urine every morning). As nursing mothers in the past would wipe their babies' faces with their wet nappies to improve their complexions, the Vernons could have been unwittingly doing themselves a lot of good by washing in water from that water butt.

[1 1]

'THOU ART PRIVY TO OUR MINUTES'

Mike Edwards of the Evesham Historical Society has written the best potted history of the privy in rhyme that I have seen. He is the only minutes secretary I have come across who produces rhyming minutes, and the following poem is a summary of a talk which I gave in Evesham in 1997.

You might think t'was kings and their armies
That shaped all the history we know,
But it seems that civilization
Is dependent much more on the flow
Of water that carries things from us
That Nature decrees we must leave;
Sometimes with a sigh of contentment,
Sometimes with a grunt and a heave.
It seems that the Ancient Egyptians
Had limestone seats on their loo
And the Cretans to stay in the fashion
Were suffering cold bottoms too.
At Housesteads the great Roman legions
Who were taking a break at the Wall,
Rushed to sit in long rows with their sponges,
Pleased at last to answer the call
Of nature, so long denied them
That constipation was rife.
We'll pass over the bogs of the Vikings
And look deeper into the life
Of ages referred to as 'Middle',

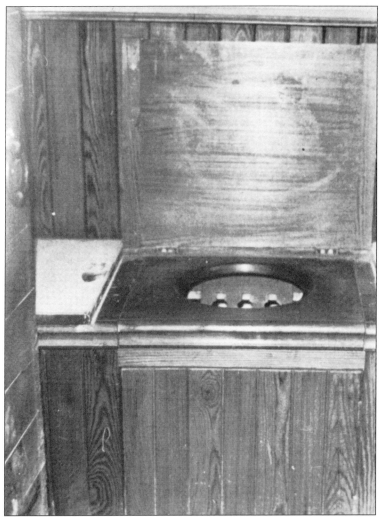

The most outstanding privy in Worcestershire – this fine mahogany seat can be found on the ground floor of the Clock Tower, known as Squire Jones's Folly, in the grounds of Abberley Hall (see over page). (Photos courtesy of Mrs Rachel Hayes)

With castles and narrow street towns
Where there's little on offer for subjects,
But close stools for those with the crowns.
There were closets to sit on in private;
There were those for the family or more!
There were Scots with large cloaks about buckets,
Whom maids in distress would implore
For relief of their pent up emotions,
And anything pent up as well.
There were gongfermors cleaning out cesspits
But on that kind of work we'll not dwell.
Harrington, Cummings and Bramah
And Crapper are names you should know,
In the study of those forms of toilet
Dependent on water flow.
The tests carried out on their functions
Would have covered both volume and weight.
There was much to be heard in the lecture
Appertaining to bowels in full spate,
But more I'm afraid I've not time for;
T'would take a complete toilet roll.
But the verdict of those who had listened
Was 'very well done – on the (w)hole!'

IN PRAISE OF THE WATER CLOSET

Thine, Lord, the Chain of Circumstance,
Beneath Thy Seat the Waters fall,
Creation's first flush Thine, for Thee
Rises and sinks the Earthly Ball.

(*J. N. Wales*)

[1 2]

TAILWINDS

George Bernard Shaw, the playwright and veteran campaigner for more public toilets for women, paid frequent visits to a teashop in Malvern and its garden privy during the 1930s. Mrs Patricia Morris of Malvern provided the following account of his visits to her mother's teashop for teas, which were served on the patch of grass in front of their bungalow on the road from The Wyche to the Worcestershire Beacon. She and her brother, Roger, used to act as guides to the visitors after their tea, as the way to the privy at the back was not straightforward. The visitors had to come through the garden gate, down some steps into a small yard and then through a shed, where her father kept a ferret in a cage, up some more steps and along a short path to the privy. Mrs Morris and her brother used to sit at a small table in the back yard with a collecting tin for pennies from duly relieved customers. She wrote: 'When visitors came out of the privy, which was brick-built and kept spotlessly clean, we would smile sweetly at them and hope that they would put a penny in our tin. A very regular visitor was George Bernard Shaw. The first time we saw him, he scared us stiff in his plus fours and his long beard. He was, however, kindness itself to us and always stopped and talked to us and would put a threepenny joey in our tin. We loved him and looked forward to his visits.'

She also added that Shaw was often accompanied by Sir Barry Jackson, who lived on the Malvern Hills and had been the driving force behind the start of the Malvern Festival in Malvern's new theatre in 1929. The 1930s were the heyday of the performance of Shaw's plays in Malvern. She ended her letter with a postscript: 'Visitors walking up the Worcestershire Beacon would often stop and admire my father's wonderful vegetable garden. The times we have heard them say, "How does he grow vegetables like that?" My brother and I would look at each other, nod our heads and go mute.' They would have upset the apple cart if they had pointed out that Shaw had made very valuable contributions.

THE GIRL GUIDE AND THE DOCTOR'S WALLET

This brave action by a girl guide happened when some North Worcestershire guides were celebrating the Queen's Silver Jubilee with a camp at Himbleton in 1977, and they were being inspected by a guide commissioner, whose husband, a well-respected doctor, accompanied her. The first thing that guides and scouts do when making camp is to dig a trench latrine. In this case chemical toilets were provided which had to be emptied into the trench. My daughter Liz was emptying one of these chemical loos when she saw a well-filled wallet slide down into the well-filled trench. Obeying the motto 'Be Prepared', she ran for a fishing net and fished for the wallet as it floated to the top of the contents of the trench. Handling the dripping wallet gingerly after netting it, she found that it belonged to the only man on the site, the commissioner's husband, who had not noticed that he had spent more than a penny when he had used the chemical loo. To my daughter's jubilation later, the doctor gave her a £5 banknote as a reward for boldly fishing where no-one had fished before, and she and her friends celebrated around the camp fire that night, singing songs of heroic deeds. She was also relieved to find that the £5 note given to her was too crisp and pristine to have been one of the sodden notes which she had rescued.

DIGGING THROUGH THE SNOW

When privies were often 20 to 40 yards away from houses, digging through snowdrifts in bad winters was heavy work. Pete Lammas, the chief reporter on the *Bromsgrove Advertiser*, remembers having to help his father dig 20 yards through snowdrifts, 5 to 6 feet deep, to reach their privy at the top of the garden in the bad winter of 1963, when they were living in Whitford. It was then open country between Whitford and Bromsgrove and the east wind blew the snow into their garden, which lay in a hollow. The wind had blown the privy door open and snow crystals covered the walls and seat, which was so sparkling that it looked like the Snow Queen's throne.

THE BOOBY TRAP

People did not usually like sharing their privies with uninvited sitters. George Stanton of Hanbury, who could turn his hand to a number of crafts, found that someone was using his garden privy on a regular basis. He decided to lay a booby trap for the cuckoo intruder by tying a stout piece of rope across the garden path leading to the privy one dark night. Unfortunately he had to pay an urgent visit to the privy the following morning and, in his hurry, forgot about his rope and fell headlong over it. He found out later that a mother and her children from Dodderhill Common had been using his privy by coming through the hedge and not along the path.

CIDER AND SAUCE!

There has been an almost symbiotic relationship between Worcestershire's production of cider, sauce and chamberpots. The county has been famous for making cider, perry and sauce which have all had powerful effects on bowel movements when consumed immoderately. The Swan public house in Chaddesley Corbett was the centre for the making of the village's perry and cider, and the annual visit of the travelling cider maker and his press is well remembered: 'Villagers, including children, would also come along with bags of apples and pears for pulping and pressing. Everyone helped with the process. Jars and small barrels were filled to take away. Fresh cider was a grand taste – but the next day was spent on the loo!"

The spectacular success of Worcestershire spicy sauce, from its first production by Lea and Perrins in 1837, encouraged one Worcester man to produce a fraudulent Worcestershire sauce. He did this by procuring all the waste materials which were put out by the Lea and Perrins factory to be collected by a local pig farmer, who was supposed to be boiling them up for his animals. The sauce made from this waste matter, stolen from the pigs, was certainly very spicy but it produced explosive movements in the bowels of the saucy forger's customers, who spent long periods on their thunder-boxes.

THE FIERY THREE-HOLE PRIVY

Ashes and cinders were commonly used to cover the unsavoury contents of pits and buckets and live embers were sometimes included. Many a wooden privy must have been burned down in the old days; even brick privies were prone to fires from this source, as Mike Hancox of Offenham has recorded: 'I well remember the earth closet at the top of my Aunt and Uncle's garden behind their house in Main Street, Offenham. They used to live in the long thatched cottages near the Maypole. The privy at the top of the garden was some 30 or 40 yards from the back door, and was screened by a large holly bush. It was always referred to as the 'Klondyke' or the 'dyke'. The dead and brittle holly leaves used to blow under the door and stick in your feet through flimsy slippers. It was mainly a brick structure about 6 feet by 4 feet with a lean-to at the back which was roughly 6 feet square. The roof was corrugated iron sheets and the scrubbed wooden seat had two large holes for adults and one smaller hole for the children. Newspaper, torn into squares and threaded on a string, hung on a nail behind the door.

'I recall how draughty it was in there, with a constant breeze being drawn like a chimney flue up through those three holes. You didn't linger longer than was absolutely necessary. The cinders and ashes were used from the fireplaces, with an occasional bag of lime to cover the waste material. Sometimes a live ember would ignite the paper content and, upon seeing clouds of smoke billowing from the lean-to, a mad panic would break out to get a bucket of water up to the closet.'

WINE-TASTING IN CLAINES

Mr Oliver Barton's grandfather used to live in a black and white timber-framed cottage in Claines with a pit privy at the bottom of his garden in a shed with two compartments, one was for the privy and the second was where he kept his home-made wine. He found that some of the bottles were being drained faster than he expected, and he suspected that some local youths were entering his store shed at night while he was asleep. He stayed up one

Richard Greatwood looks into the old pit privy at Old House Farm, Hanbury.

night and crept down the garden path and locked the thieves in the wine store. He then broke the skin which had formed on his cesspit in the privy next door and released the noxious fumes like an evil genie set free from a bottle. Sounds of violent retching and vomiting soon emanated from the trapped thieves, who were let out in a pitiful condition after a suitable period of incarceration with those stinking gases. They never returned for another wine-tasting; the bouquet was too fruity.

TWO ROMSLEY LOOS

An Elsan chemical loo now stands in the crypt of St Kenelm's church in Romsley, less than 3 feet away from the spot where the young Prince Kenelm of Mercia was murdered in AD 819, according to several monastic writers. When his body was discovered at Cowbatch in the Clent Hills, a holy spring with miraculous healing properties began to rise from that place. Thousands of pilgrims travelled every year to bathe in St Kenelm's spring and it became one of the holiest shrines in the country. St Kenelm's church was built over the spring, which was roofed over by the crypt and was directly under the chancel. The spring has now been diverted to flow from lower down the hill, but sitting on the loo in the crypt is a powerful reminder of where the original spring bubbled up. The village of Kenelmstowe grew up around the church in the Middle Ages to cater for the needs of the pilgrims, but their privy arrangements are not recorded.

Another unusual privy in Romsley used to be the two-holer outside the Primitive Methodist Chapel which was built in 1870. It was unusual because most Nonconformist churches were not built with privies in the 19th century, and this was a spectacular two-holer with one seat for adults and a lower one for children. Many Anglican churches also had no privies so the long sermons of Victorian times were often agonising. St Kenelm's did not have its Elsan loo until recent years. Romsley's historian, Joe Hunt, recalled the Methodist privy very clearly because it was his job as a boy to fold and string newspapers for it. He added: 'There was a small garden at the rear of the privy which was rented to a villager and we often wondered at the size and quality of his fruit and vegetables.' Clearly the holy spring was still working its miracles.

FLUSHED BY THE CANAL

Lane House Farm in Alvechurch was one of the first farms in Worcestershire to convert its privy into a water closet, long before it had any mains water supply. The Worcester and Birmingham Canal was cut through its land and in exchange for this concession the Canal Company allowed water from the canal to be piped by gravity feed to the farmhouse, where it was used to flush the outside water closet and for washing. Drinking water for the farm came from a well by the back door, or, if the well failed, from the farm's cottage which was connected to the mains water supply long before the farmhouse.

When the farm's water closet failed to flush, it was usually because the inlet pipe from the canal had become blocked. Miss V. Greaves gave the following graphic account of the cold and uncomfortable lengths to which members of her family had to go in order to restore a lost flush: 'When the inlet from the canal got blocked, you went onto the towpath (via a stile), removed the turf and the wooden cover under it, to get at the inlet, a thick lead pipe with holes in it. You then lay face down on the bank, with your arm in water up to the shoulder, to clear stones and debris from the holes. After which you replaced the cover and turf. We also had our own sewer. All the waste water and effluent from the lavatory, house and outbuildings ran through pipes to a deep sock pit, which was covered and emptied by pumping into a horse-drawn tank. The tank went into the fields, spraying the liquid manure as fertiliser. The run-off from the muck heap also went into the sock pit.'

Many lock keepers' cottages had privies which were converted to water closets in the early 20th century, with sewer pipes emptying the sewage directly into the canals. The outlets for the pipes were placed near the lock gates, where there was more turbulent water for the quick dispersal of waste matter.

LOO PAPER AND LITERACY

'Sitting on the loo with a newspaper is a leisure activity for many men.' (*A feminist*)

The connection between loo paper and reading would make a serious subject for academic research. It is arguable that the decline in literacy among some sections in the population is directly related to the spread of blank manufactured loo paper since the Second World War. Before the 1950s the printed word was to be found in most privies and WCs, in the form of newspapers, which were often cut into squares and hung on nails, and some of this print was duly transferred to the fundament.

Bill Kings, Bromsgrove's most venerable historian, has described how the shared two-hole privy in Crawford's Yard or Court, behind the town's High Street, was an early website of shared information over 80 years ago. His family lived in one of six cottages which shared this privy, and they also shared one copy of the *News of the World*, which each family took it in turns to buy. His grandfather, Jack Kings, who was a nailer, and Charlie Holliday, a chimney sweep, always had to be first to read the communal paper, and they perused it sitting side by side on the communal two-holer every Sunday morning. During the rest of the week they would read snippets aloud to the many people who could not read in that yard. It was Bill Kings' job as a lad to cut the newspaper into squares and string them up on the back of the door. He said that it was straining to read those squares in the privy which gave him the stimulus to start reading by the age of four.

I still remember my extensive reading in our outside WC before I reached twelve years of age, beginning with comics like the *Beano* and *Dandy* when I was five and the *Wizard* and *Hotspur* a few years later, graduating to the very literate *Magnet* and *Gem*.

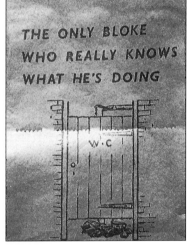

Printed lavatory paper from the 1930s. (Poultney Collection)

Now I rely on authors like Herodotus, Bill Bryson, Alan Coren, P. G. Wodehouse and Conan Doyle to accompany me to the inner sanctum.

It is only right and proper that Worcestershire, as a major manufacturer of chamberpots, can claim to have more lavatorial place names than most counties. Wyre Piddle is the best known of these, and one Worcestershire wine was once marked with that village's name. There was an attempt to remove the offending 'Piddle' from the name in 1905, which fortunately failed. Piddle Brook still flows through Wyre Piddle and Lower Piddle. There is another water village on the Severn called Ripple, and ancient field names in the Kinver area include Little Wigley, Big Wigley, Giants Well Piece and Slash.

TAILPIECE

Pee, poo, pong, plop,
From the press a privy book.
For this relief I give much thanks;
Go little book and fare thee well!

A PRIVY ALPHABET

A is for the Ash-pit, where people chuck it.
B is for Bog, Baby Blake or Bucket.
C is for Chamberpot, the famous guzunder.
D is for Dunny, as known in Downunder.
E is for Easement, a place of ease.
F is for Flushing in order to please.
G Gents and Gong house in which men browse.
H is for Heads in front of the bows.
I is for Iron Duke, the night-soil cart.
Full to overflowing, it played its part.
J is for Jerry, Jakes, Jordan and John.
K is for Khazi we all sit upon.
L is for Lavatory, Latrine and Loo.
M is for Moule; earth covers the stool.
N is for Number Two's and Netty,
Number 100 in Europe and Turkey.
O is for Offices where ordure was dropped,
And load after load of manure can be cropped.
P is for Pissoir, Pan and Privy,
Ping-pong House and Porcelain Pony.
Q Quality of stools show the state of our health.
R is the Reredorter where monks went by stealth.
S is for Shithouse, Superloo and Shot-tower.
T is for Thunder-box if we lived in Goa.
U is Up-the-yard, Umtag in Russia.
V is for Vespasiennes in France, much lusher.
W is for Wee house in Wyre Piddle.
X marks the spot where they do their widdle.
Y is Yer Tiz and You Know Where.
Z is for Zero-gravity toilet; of them beware!

Sheila Richards

ACKNOWLEDGEMENTS

In addition to those who feature in the stories and photographs on these pages, I would like to thank the following for their help. Firstly Michael Thomas, the former Director of Avoncroft Museum, who passed on to me the many letters and photographs which he had collected when he was planning to write this book; Max Harper, the Stoke Prior photographer, who took many additional photographs for me, often in risky situations on the tops of walls and rickety ladders after plodding through very muddy farms; Norman Neason, RWS, RBSA, the Redditch artist who has illustrated most of my books, has again provided several drawings, based on his memory of farms in Worcestershire where several generations of his family have farmed. I was very fortunate to be able to include photographs of items in the Poultney Collection. Bernard and Olive Poultney of Sharpway Gate, Stoke Prior, not only have the most picturesque wooden privy in the county, but also an unrivalled knowledge of privies in the Hanbury and Stoke Prior area, together with a large collection of photographs. They were indefatigable in the quest for privies and artefacts in their locality. Thanks also to Pete Lammas, chief reporter of the *Bromsgrove Advertiser*, who was an enthusiastic source of information. I am also indebted to the Worcestershire Federation of Women's Institutes whose book, *Worcestershire Within Living Memory*, was a valuable source of information. Finally I would like to thank three of my daughters, Virginia, Jennifer and Alison for chauffeuring me around the county in the great privy quest, and my wife Sheila for being my soundest critic.